The Daddy's Girl devotional

A Prayer, Planning & Activity Journal for Girls

JENNY ERLINGSSON
WITH NYEMA ERLINGSSON

www.milkandhoneybooks.com

Copyright © 2020 by Jenny Erlingsson, Nyema Erlingsson

All rights reserved. This book is protected by copyright laws of the United States of America. This book may not be copied or reprinted for commercial gain or profit. The use of short quotations or occasional page copying for personal or group study is permitted and encouraged. Permission will be granted upon request.

Scripture quotations marked (NIV) are taken from the Holy Bible, New International Version®, NIV®. Copyright © 1973, 1978, 1984, 2011 by Biblica, Inc.™ Used by permission of Zondervan. All rights reserved worldwide. www.zondervan.com The "NIV" and "New International Version" are trademarks registered in the United States Patent and Trademark Office by Biblica, Inc.™

Scripture quotations marked (NLT) are taken from the Holy Bible, New Living Translation, copyright ©1996, 2004, 2015 by Tyndale House Foundation. Used by permission of Tyndale House Publishers, a Division of Tyndale House Ministries, Carol Stream, Illinois 60188. All rights reserved.

Scripture quotations marked (ERV) are taken from the Holy Bible: Easy-to-Read Version (ERV), International Edition© 2013, 2016 by Bible League International and used by permission. All Rights Reserved.

This book is available at:
Cover & Interior Design by Jenny Erlingsson via Canva

Reach us on the Internet: milkandhoneybooks.com or milkandhoneywomen.com
ISBN TP: 978-1-953000-00-2

For Worldwide Distribution, Printed in the United States of America
1 2 3 4 5 6 7 8 9 10

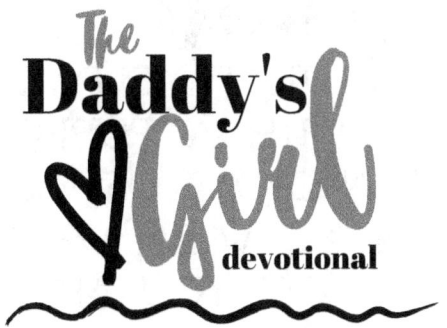

THIS BOOK BELONGS TO:

....

www.milkandhoneywomen.com

Hey Sweet Girl!

DID YOU KNOW THAT YOU WERE CREATED ON PURPOSE AND WITH A PURPOSE? GOD LOVES YOU SO MUCH AND ONE OF THE BEST THINGS WE GET TO BE CALLED WHEN WE KNOW JESUS IS A DAUGHTER OF GOD. YOU ARE A DADDY'S GIRL. THIS JOURNAL IS ALL ABOUT YOU AND HOW MUCH GOD LOVES YOU AND HOW WE CAN SHOW OTHERS HOW MUCH WE LOVE HIM. WE HOPE THAT YOU WILL USE THIS BOOK TO DRAW & DREAM & WRITE & READ & COLOR AS YOU SPEND WITH JESUS. HE LOVES YOU SO MUCH. HE PAID A BIG PRICE FOR YOU AND HE WANTS YOU TO KNOW THAT YOU BELONG TO HIM. IF YOU NEED HELP WITH ANY PART, ASK SOMEONE OLDER TO HELP YOU.

HAVE FUN! ♡ Jenny & Nyema (Jenny's oldest daughter)

Your Heart Belongs to Jesus

If there is a grown up girl in your life, tell them to check out Milk & Honey Women for more books, blogs, & inspiration just for them.

Come. Taste & see

WWW.MILKANDHONEYWOMEN.COM

Week 1

In the beginning, God created everything.

Week 1

OUR AMAZING CREATOR

God is an amazing creator. In the beginning of all things it was His words that set things in motion. When he spoke, light shot forth, the sun, moon and stars came into existence. But the best thing that God created wasn't the stars in the sky, the mountains or the oceans. It wasn't even the cutest puppy or the strongest elephant. The best of God's creation is you and me. God created us to watch and rule over the earth but most of all, He created us to love Him and know Him.

What are some things in creation that make you smile? Are there any plants, animals, or landscapes that make you think about God?

Write Your Thoughts

_____

_____

_____

_____

_____

 **MONDAY** | **My Week** | **TUESDAY**

WEDNESDAY | **THURSDAY**

Bible Verse

In the beginning God created the heavens and the earth. Now the earth was formless and empty, darkness was over the surface of the deep, and the Spirit of God was hovering over the waters. And God said, "Let there be light," and there was light.
Genesis 1:1-3 NIV

FRIDAY

SATURDAY

SUNDAY

EVE

The one who was first
Genesis 2:4-25; 3:1-24

Eve was the first woman that God created. God created Adam, whose name means "mankind" from the dust of the ground and breathed his breath of life into Him. The Bible says that God took a piece of Adam and formed Eve. He made Eve as a perfect helper to Adam. This doesn't mean that she was less than or behind him. It means that she was created in the image of God too and also had the responsibility to work alongside Adam in taking care of the earth. But most of all, she was created to be friends with God.

The Bible says that God walked with Adam and Eve in the cool of the day. Even when they messed up and sinned, God made a plan to fix it. He loved spending time with Adam & Eve. And he loves spending time with you.

What are ways that you can spend time with God today?

Write Your Thoughts

_____

_____

_____

_____

What are some of your favorite things that God created?

Week 1

what else?

Week 1

In the beginning God created the heavens and the earth. Now the earth was formless and empty, darkness was over the surface of the deep, and the Spirit of God was hovering over the waters. And God said, "Let there be light," and there was light.

Genesis 1:1-3 NIV

Week 2

God Loves Me. He did a good job making me.

Week 2

I AM WONDERFULLY MADE

God has a specific plan and purpose for you and that includes how He made you. He looks at you and sees His beautiful daughter. Sometimes when we look in the mirror we don't always feel that way. Maybe you are shorter or taller than others. Or maybe you don't walk the same or even talk the same. Sometimes we are even born with abilities that make us have to do things a little differently.

God doesn't want you to feel bad about how He made you. He wants you to see yourself the way He sees you. There are so many special gifts that he has given to just YOU. You have value because He sent His most valuable One to you. He sent Jesus to remind us how priceless and beautiful we are. **What are some things that are special about you?**

Write Your Thoughts

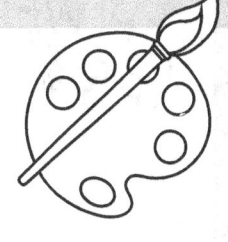

_____

_____

_____

_____

_____

 MONDAY

My Week

TUESDAY

WEDNESDAY

THURSDAY

Bible Verse

I praise you because you made me in such a wonderful way. I know how amazing that was!

Psalm 139:14 ERV

FRIDAY

SATURDAY

SUNDAY

SHIPRAH & PUAH

The ones who were brave
Exodus 1:15-21

There was a time in the Bible that was very sad for so many people. God made a promise to Abraham and his wife Sarah that he would make a great group of people through their son Isaac. Out of this people he would bring someone who would change the world. As Abraham's people grew larger and stronger they ended up in Egypt and after many years they had to become slaves! The leaders in Egypt were so afraid of how strong God's people were they told the two women responsible for helping moms deliver babies, to get rid of any boys they saw.

But these women were very brave and they did not kill any baby boys like Pharaoh told them to. They knew that those lives were precious and valuable to God, no matter how small. God blessed them because of their good choices. **How can you make a good, brave choice today?**

Write Your Thoughts

_____

_____

_____

_____

DRAW SOMETHING THAT MAKES YOU UNIQUE, STRONG OR BRAVE

Week 2

Week 2

I praise you because you made me in such a wonderful way. I know how AMAZING that was!
Psalm 139:14 ERV

Week 3

When I was far away, God sent Jesus for me.

Week 3

GOD'S RESCUE PLAN

At the beginning Adam and Eve were meant to walk in deep friendship with God. But that friendship was broken when Adam & Eve were tempted and made the choice to sin. Sin is more than doing the wrong thing. Sin is what we do against God's commands and it keeps us from God.

But God made a plan of rescue before any of us were born. He sent his son Jesus in the form of a baby, to grow up, walk with us, teach us and be with us. He came so that we would have a bridge back to His Father. **Have you asked Jesus to come into your life, forgive you of your sins and bring you back to God?** If not, there is no better time than now to do that. Just pray to God. Ask Jesus to forgive you of your sins and ask Him to enter your life and make you new.

Write Your Thoughts

_____

_____

_____

_____

_____

 MONDAY | My Week | TUESDAY

WEDNESDAY | THURSDAY

Bible Verse

Yes, God loved the world so much that he gave his only Son, so that everyone who believes in him would not be lost but have eternal life.
John 3:16 ERV

FRIDAY

SATURDAY

SUNDAY

The one who took care of Jesus
Luke 1:26-38

Mary was just a normal young woman living in Israel. Like other Jewish people, she was waiting for the day their hero would come. He was called the Messiah, the Anointed One and He would rescue their people from all the bad things going on in their lives.

One day Mary had the surprise of her life when an angel appeared to her! This messenger told her that she was so special to God in Heaven and that she was chosen to be the carrier of the promised Messiah. Just like at creation, God's Holy Spirit would cover her, giving her the ability to give birth to the Savior. He was God's rescue plan for the entire world. Even now, when we have Jesus in our lives, we carry Him to everyone around us.

Who can you "carry" Jesus to today?

Write Your Thoughts

_____

_____

_____

_____

Week 3

Yes, God loved the world so much that he gave his only Son, so that everyone who believes in him would not be lost but have eternal life.
John 3:16 ERV

love

Week 4

Jesus paid the price that I could not pay.

Week 4

THE BEST GIFT

Have you ever wanted something so badly but it cost more money than you had? It may feel impossible to get it. In a similar way, because of sin people are away from God and are not able to pay the great price needed to wash away all of their sins. In the past, people used animal sacrifices, but when Jesus came to earth He came to pay the price that we couldn't pay. Even though none of it was His fault, he put all the blame on his shoulders so that we wouldn't have to.

Jesus gave us the gift of salvation. Remember that thing you wanted? Imagine that someone gave it to you as a gift. You would be so thankful for that gift because you knew you couldn't buy it for yourself. **How can you show your thanks to Jesus, for the great gift that He's given to you?**

Write Your Thoughts

_____
_____
_____
_____

 MONDAY | My Week | TUESDAY

WEDNESDAY | THURSDAY

Bible Verse

When people sin, they earn what sin pays—death. But God gives his people a free gift—eternal life in Christ Jesus our Lord.
Romans 6:23 ERV

FRIDAY

SATURDAY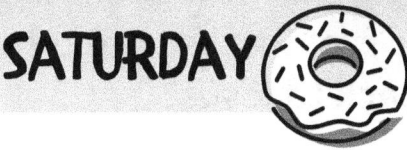

SUNDAY

MARY OF BETHANY

The one who was friends with Jesus
John 12:1-6

Mary lived with her sister and brother in a town called Bethany. These siblings were good friends of Jesus. There were many people and twelve disciples that followed Jesus but He often visited their house. They cooked, laughed and talked together. One day, there was a dinner that took place with this family in attendance.

Mary had a special oil in a beautiful box that cost a lot of money. She could have used it to buy lots of other things but instead she wanted to give it as a gift. She gave it to Jesus by breaking it open and pouring that sweet smell on his feet, and she even finished cleaning his feet with her hair. She believed He was the true King and the Messiah. She recognized that Jesus came to bring them a wonderful gift and she wanted to give her own gift of thanks in return. **Is there something you can give back to Jesus?**

Write Your Thoughts

_____

_____

_____

_____

WHAT ARE SOME OF THE GIFTS YOU CAN GIVE BACK TO JESUS IN WORSHIP?

Week 4

1.

2.

3.

4.

Week 4

WHEN PEOPLE SIN, THEY EARN WHAT SIN PAYS—DEATH. BUT GOD GIVES HIS PEOPLE A FREE GIFT—ETERNAL LIFE IN CHRIST JESUS OUR LORD.
ROMANS 6:23

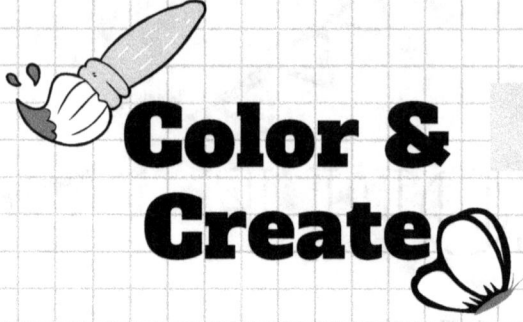

Week 5

I am made brand new & promised life in heaven that will never end.

Week 5

BRAND NEW

After Jesus gave us the gift of salvation by dying on the cross, he came back to life after three days. Through his resurrection we have new, eternal life. When we know Jesus, we are not the same person we were before Jesus.

All the dirty sin has been washed away and we are a new creation. God comes into our lives and creates our hearts brand new, just like He did at creation. Because of this new life we can live in new ways. We can pray to God and talk with Him. We can say no to the things that are not like God.

What is exciting to you about being a new creation in Jesus?

Write Your Thoughts

_____

_____

_____

_____

_____

_____

 MONDAY   My Week   TUESDAY

WEDNESDAY   THURSDAY

Bible Verse

Therefore, if anyone is in Christ, the new creation has come: The old has gone, the new is here!
2 Corinthians 5:17 ERV

FRIDAY

SATURDAY

SUNDAY

The one Jesus set free
Luke 8:1-3; 24:1-12

Mary Magdalene was a woman who followed very closely after Jesus. But it wasn't always this way for her. Before she met Jesus, she lived a life of a lot of fear. We don't know what happened in her life but we know that she was bothered and controlled by evil spirits.

This was not what God wanted for her life. The Bible says that Jesus set her free and after that, she became a faithful follower of Jesus. She was completely changed and no longer afraid. She stayed around Jesus all the way up to the cross and after He rose again, she got to be the first one to tell others that He was alive!

What is something Jesus has made new in your life?

Write Your Thoughts

_____

_____

_____

_____

_____

THERE ARE A LOT OF WOMEN THAT HAVE FORMS OF THE NAME "MARY" IN THE BIBLE. CAN YOU MATCH THEM TO OBJECTS FROM THEIR STORIES?

Week 5

Matching Marys

1 **Mary of Bethany**
(BOOK OF JOHN/CH. 12)

WHEAT

2 **Mary, Mother of Jesus**
(BOOK OF LUKE)

TAMBOURINE

3 **Mary Magdalene**
(BOOK OF JOHN/CH. 20)

CONTAINER OF OIL

4 **Miriam, sister of Moses**
(BOOK OF EXODUS)

THE CROSS

5 **Mara, also known as Naomi**
(BOOK OF RUTH)

MANGER

ANSWERS: 1-OIL, 2-MANGER, 3-CROSS, 4-TAMBOURINE, 5-WHEAT

Week 6

I am a daughter of God. I can be close to Him.

CLOSE TO GOD

When we know Jesus, we are invited to be close to Father God. Everything that kept us from God is gone. And you know what is so beautiful about this friendship? We are brought into the family of God and are called daughters of God. Just like in the first garden when Adam and Eve were a son and daughter of God. This is such a sweet name that God gives us because it means that no matter what is happening in our lives we belong to Him. Even if you have no parents, or one parent, or live with your grandparents, or someone else, you can always know that you have a place with God because He calls you His daughter. And that means you can always run to Him for whatever you need.

Is there something even now that you want to ask your Father in Heaven for?

Write Your Thoughts

_____

_____

_____

_____

_____

 MONDAY   My Week   TUESDAY

WEDNESDAY   THURSDAY

Bible Verse

With Jesus as our high priest, we can feel free to come before God's throne where there is grace. There we receive mercy and kindness to help us when we need it.
Hebrews 4:16 ERV

FRIDAY

SATURDAY

SUNDAY

WOMAN WHO WAS BLEEDING

The one Jesus healed
Matthew 9:20, Mark 5:25-34, Luke 8:43-48

There is a woman in the Bible who was sick for a long time. We don't know her name but we know that she wanted to be healed very badly. She spent all her money going to doctors until she was poor and alone. One day she heard that Jesus was in town so she tried her hardest to make it to Him. The crowd was so big that it was hard to get close to Him. But she had big faith and knew that if she could just touch Him a little bit, she would be healed.

She reached out and touched the edge of his clothing and she was completely healed! But the best part happened next. Jesus looked around for her and when He found her he told her that her she was healed and then he called her daughter. Jesus wanted her to know that she belonged to him and that she wasn't alone anymore. She was so loved by Him and so are you! **What does it mean to you to be a daughter of God?**

Write Your Thoughts

_____

_____

_____

_____

GOD IS STRONG ENOUGH TO TAKE CARE OF EVERYTHING

Week 6

How does God help when you are afraid?

What can you do when you are worried?

What makes you laugh?

What is your favorite thing to do?

What do you do that makes God smile?

What do you need help with this week?

Week 6

With Jesus as our high priest, we can feel free to come before God's throne where there is grace. There we receive mercy and kindness to help us when we need it.

Hebrews 4:16 ERV

Week 7

Everything Jesus has, He wants to give me too

A ROYAL PRINCESS

Week 7

Knowing Jesus means being born again into God's Kingdom. That makes you a princess in his kingdom. A princess knows that she is loved and cared for. Think about the prince and princesses you read about in stories or even see from different countries. They know that they are very important to the countries they serve. They are treasured and the King and Queen have everything that they need.

Being a princess in God's kingdom means the same thing but so much more. Jesus has all the power and rules over everything . When we know Jesus, we can ask for everything he has for us. God wants us to dream big and to dream with Him to see the world changed all around us.

What is something in your life that you want to see God change?

Write Your Thoughts

_____

_____

_____

_____

_____

 MONDAY   My Week   TUESDAY

WEDNESDAY   THURSDAY

Bible Verse

We know who he is, and we know who we are: Father and children. And we know we are going to get what's coming to us—an unbelievable inheritance! We go through exactly what Christ goes through. If we go through the hard times with him, then we're certainly going to go through the good times with him!

Romans 8:17 MSG

FRIDAY

SATURDAY

SUNDAY

SARAH

The one called princess
Genesis 12:10-20, Genesis 15-17, Genesis 18:1-15

Sarah was a woman who got to be a part of a big rescue plan that God had for the world. Abraham and Sarah were trusted by God to be the start of a chosen people. They would be the parents of a great nation that would help the whole world. But there were times that Sarah didn't believe that God could use her. She felt like she was too old to have a child and that God would not do what He said He would.

But God reminded Sarah that nothing was impossible with Him. In fact, her name used to be Sarai, but He gave her the name of Sarah, which means "Princess". God reminded her that she was the daughter of the King who was able to do anything. God made promises with them that still go on today. Part of that promise is Jesus, who was born through Abraham & Sarah's family. **Are there any promises that you need help remembering?**

Write Your Thoughts

_____

_____

_____

_____

WHAT ARE SOME THINGS THAT YOU HOPE & DREAM FOR?

Week 7

Week 8

Jesus sent the Holy Spirit to live in me and help me.

OUR SPECIAL HELPER

Week 8

Before Jesus went back to Heaven He told the disciples that He would send them a comforter, a special helper that would give them power to be more like Jesus. The Holy Spirit lives inside of us. We don't ever have to feel lonely or be afraid because He reminds us of God's love for us and the gift of salvation Jesus gave us.

Sometimes it's hard to understand how this happens but think about yourself. You are a whole person that is made up of many layers. You are **1.)** body **2.)** soul (mind, thoughts & feelings) and **3.)** heart (spirit). So when we believe in Jesus, God the Son, we get to be close to God the Father and be the house for God, the Holy Spirit. **What do you need the Holy Spirit to help you with today?**

Write Your Thoughts

_____

_____

_____

_____

_____

 MONDAY

My Week

TUESDAY

WEDNESDAY

THURSDAY

Bible Verse

Since you are now God's children, he has sent the Spirit of his Son into your hearts. The Spirit cries out,
" Abba, Father."
Galatians 4:6 ERV

FRIDAY

SATURDAY

SUNDAY

JAIRUS' DAUGHTER

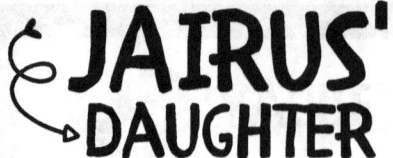

The one who was sick
Matthew 9:20, Mark 5:25-34, Luke 8:43-48

A couple lessons ago we talked about a woman that was sick for a long time. At the same time that she went to Jesus for healing, there was a little girl who was also sick. Her daddy went to Jesus to ask Him to heal his daughter. By the time Jesus got to the house, the little girl died. But Jesus wasn't afraid or unsure of what to do. He was filled and overflowing with the Holy Spirit and He knew that He could bring life back to her body. And you know what? He did! This same Holy Spirit brought life back to *His* body when He came back to life. The Holy Spirit can bring life to all the dark, dead and sad places around you.

Think about this special verse:

"God raised Jesus from death. And if God's Spirit lives in you, he will also give life to your bodies that die. Yes, God is the one who raised Christ from death, and he will raise you to life through his Spirit living in you." Romans 8:11 ERV

Write Your Thoughts

_____

_____

_____

_____

WHEN JESUS RAISED JAIRUS' DAUGHTER TO LIFE, HE TOLD HER FAMILY TO GIVE HER FOOD TO EAT.

Week 8

WHAT ARE SOME OF YOUR FAVORITE FOODS?
CAN YOU FIND THE PANCAKES, TACOS, HAMBURGER, WATERMELON, DOUGHNUT & APPLE?

Week 8

"SINCE YOU ARE NOW GOD'S CHILDREN, HE HAS SENT THE SPIRIT OF HIS SON INTO YOUR HEARTS. THE SPIRIT CRIES OUT, "ABBA, FATHER.""

GALATIANS 4:6 ERV

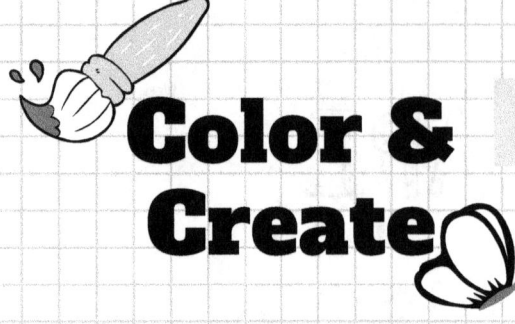

Week 9

Holy Spirit helps me live a life that makes Him smile.

LISTENING TO GOD

Living our lives for Jesus is the best choice we can make but it's not always easy. There are so many things that may take our attention away from God. This is why Jesus wants us to have the Holy Spirit as a helper. The Holy Spirit begins to lead us through the Bible, when we pray, when we worship and especially when we lean close and listen to Him. Many times He speaks to us in a still small voice that we hear in our hearts because He wants us to get quiet and focused enough to listen. Even when we feel like God is telling us no, we can trust that its because He loves us and has a better plan for us. When we turn off the television or games or take time away from playing to spend time with Him, we get filled with all that we need to live a life that makes God smile. **What do you need to do (or turn off) to help you listen to God better?**

Write Your Thoughts

_____

_____

_____

_____

_____

 MONDAY **My Week** TUESDAY

WEDNESDAY THURSDAY

Bible Verse

So I tell you, live the way the Spirit leads you. Then you will not do the evil things your sinful self wants.
Galatians 5:16 ERV

FRIDAY

SATURDAY

SUNDAY

MARTHA

The one Jesus helped choose well
Luke 10:38-42

Do you remember us talking about Mary a few weeks ago? Martha was her sister and was also friends with Jesus. Martha was always very busy preparing food for Jesus and his disciples. She really wanted her sister to help her cook and not sit and listen to Jesus. This story about Martha is special because in it we see Jesus show her how to make better choices. But Jesus wanted to remind Martha that spending time with Him is more important than all the things we do. This doesn't mean that we stop listening to our parents or other leaders, but it means that we should always make sure our days start, end and circle around Jesus. Jesus wants to be a part of everything we do, not away from it. **How can you make sure Jesus is always a part of what YOU do?**

Write Your Thoughts

_____

_____

_____

_____

_____

MARTHA DOES A LOT OF GOOD THINGS BUT HELP HER GET TO JESUS WITHOUT GETTING DISTRACTED!

Week 9

"Martha, Martha, you are getting worried and upset about too many things. Only one thing is important."
Luke 10:41-42a ERV

Week 9

So I tell you, live the way the Spirit leads you. Then you will not do the evil things your sinful self wants.

Galatians 5:16 ERV

Week 10

My God is so strong and He is so Good.

Week 10

WE CAN TRUST HIM

Many times we see so many hard things happen around us and we may not feel like we are strong or powerful enough to do something. This is why its so important to remember that you are a daughter of God because of what Jesus did for you on the cross. Even though we may not be the strongest or the smartest or richest or even bravest, our Father God is. He is the strongest, bravest, smartest, richest and He will take care of all the things that we give to Him. He cares about what we care about, from the smallest to the biggest thing. He also loves being with you and having fun with you. We can trust that we are safe and protected by Him and this should bring us all kinds of joy.

What is something fun you can do with God today?

Write Your Thoughts

_____

_____

_____

_____

_____

 MONDAY   My Week   TUESDAY

WEDNESDAY   THURSDAY

Bible Verse

The Lord your God is with you. He is like a powerful soldier. He will save you. He will show how much he loves you and how happy he is with you. He will laugh and be happy about you,
Zephaniah 3:17 ERV

FRIDAY

SATURDAY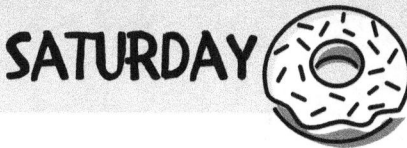

SUNDAY

MIRIAM
The one who saved her brother
Exodus 2:1-10, Exodus 15:20-21

Miriam was a part of the Hebrew people that were slaves in Egypt. We talked about them a few weeks ago in the story of Shiprah and Puah. Even though the midwives made the right choice to not kill any of the Hebrew boys, Pharaoh still wanted to continue his plans. Miriam had a baby brother named Moses who was in danger. But because of her quick thinking and bravery she helped save her brother from death. She also made sure that her mother could still be a part of his life. Many years later, when that same brother delivered their people from Egypt, Miriam led the women in singing and dancing with her tambourine, praising God for all He had done.

What is something brave you have done because you trusted in God?

Write Your Thoughts

_____

_____

_____

_____

FIND THE WORDS THAT HELP YOU REMEMBER OUR VERSE

Week 10

```
T P H M Y A W T V Y O J F
V L H U I U Q H R W A K Q Y A
Z U A Q N M A P C T I C H N D
T E P U Z S W S O L D I E R L
K N P K X D T P I W V A M K O
M A Y H O X Z O H D E W Y A M
H I C O A N T X P M D R X J N
S A G O J N O M U P B X F I I
F T S H L V I X L T A M W U Y
G S R O T O R A V G K B S S L
P A Y O R Y V R H B M W L P F
Y V Y B N C P E R X G J J E K
G I L A U G H T E R C Q Q Y I
U O U M N V H I E Z V L F H N
U R D G R D Z J M C K V V N D
```

STRONG
POWERFUL
MIGHTY
KIND
GOOD
UNSTOPPABLE

SAVIOR
HAPPY
SOLDIER
LOVE
LAUGHTER
ZEPHANIAH

The Lord your God is with you. He is like a powerful soldier. He will save you. He will show how much he loves you and how happy he is with you. He will laugh and be happy about you,
Zephaniah 3:17 ERV

Week 11

Jesus can do amazing things in my life and in the lives of others.

Week 11

NOTHING IS IMPOSSIBLE

The Bible is full of so many stories where God did amazing things in the lives of the people who knew Him. He brought healing, increased food, set people free from demons and even raised some from the dead. And isn't it cool that God never changes? That means the things He did back then, He can do and does now. The name of Jesus is more powerful than any other name around and when we speak His name and believe in Him, nothing can stand up against Him. There may be things going on in your life that seem dark or fearful or painful. But never forget that nothing is impossible with God and that your faith in Jesus can accomplish great things. **What is something really amazing that you are praying for?**

Write Your Thoughts

_____

_____

_____

_____

_____

My Week

MONDAY

TUESDAY

WEDNESDAY

THURSDAY

Bible Verse

God can do anything!

Luke 1:37 ERV

FRIDAY

SATURDAY

SUNDAY

NAAMAN'S SERVANT
The one who helped her enemy
2 Kings 5

There was a young girl in the Bible who went through a lot of painful things. During a time of war, she was captured and ended up as the servant of the general of the enemy army. Even though she was away from her family and friends, she was never away from God.

The general had a disease that caused him lots of pain and trouble. Because this girl was close to God, she had God's heart for this man. She told him that her God could heal him and that the prophet Elisha could pray for his healing. The general did what she said and after he visited the prophet and did what he was told to do, he was healed!! **Many times a big miracle is when you do good to someone who has done wrong to you. How can you do the same in your life?**

Write Your Thoughts

_____

_____

_____

_____

_____

IMAGINE WHAT THE FISHES SAW WHEN NAAMAN WAS HEALED!

Week 11

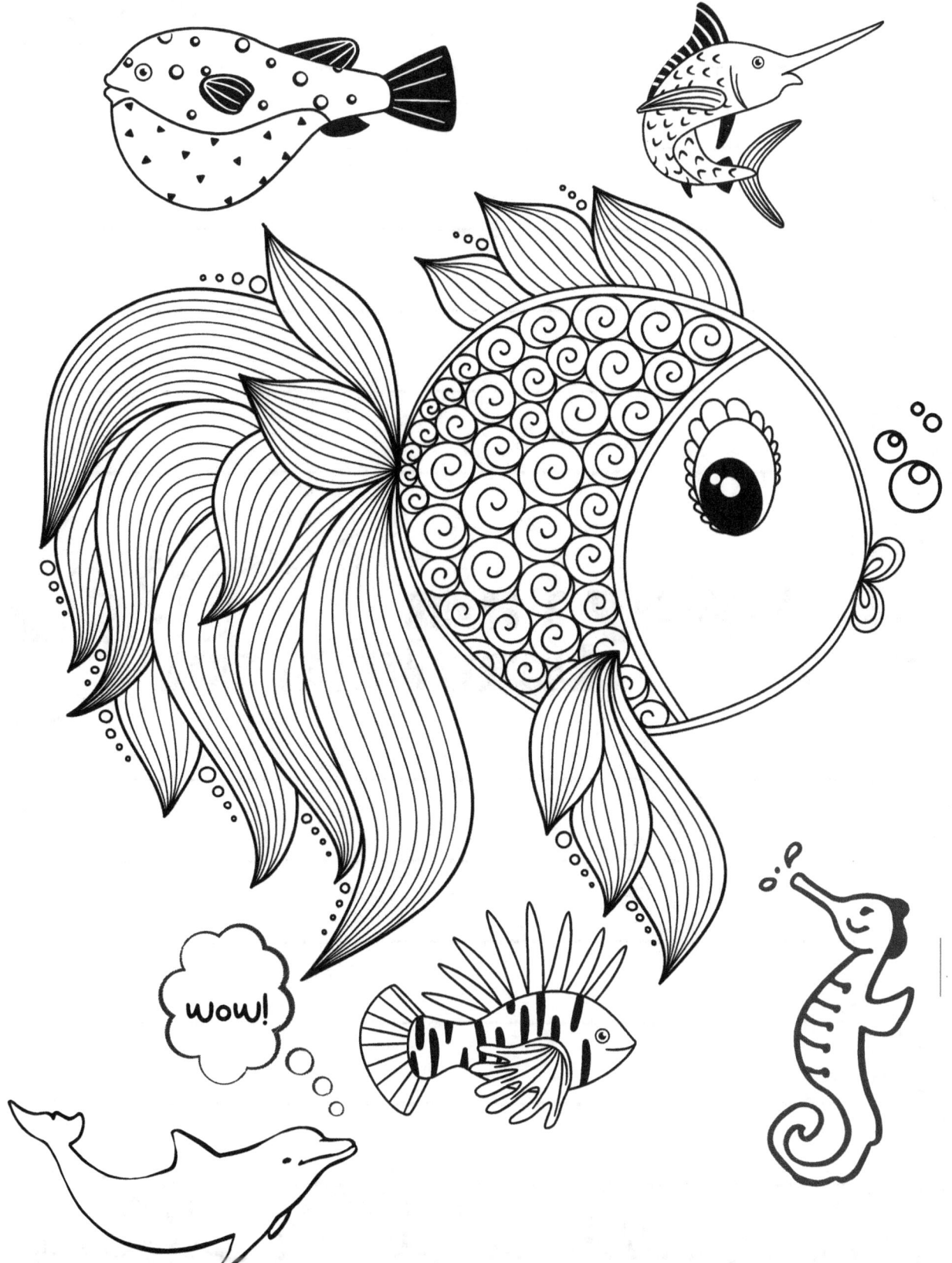

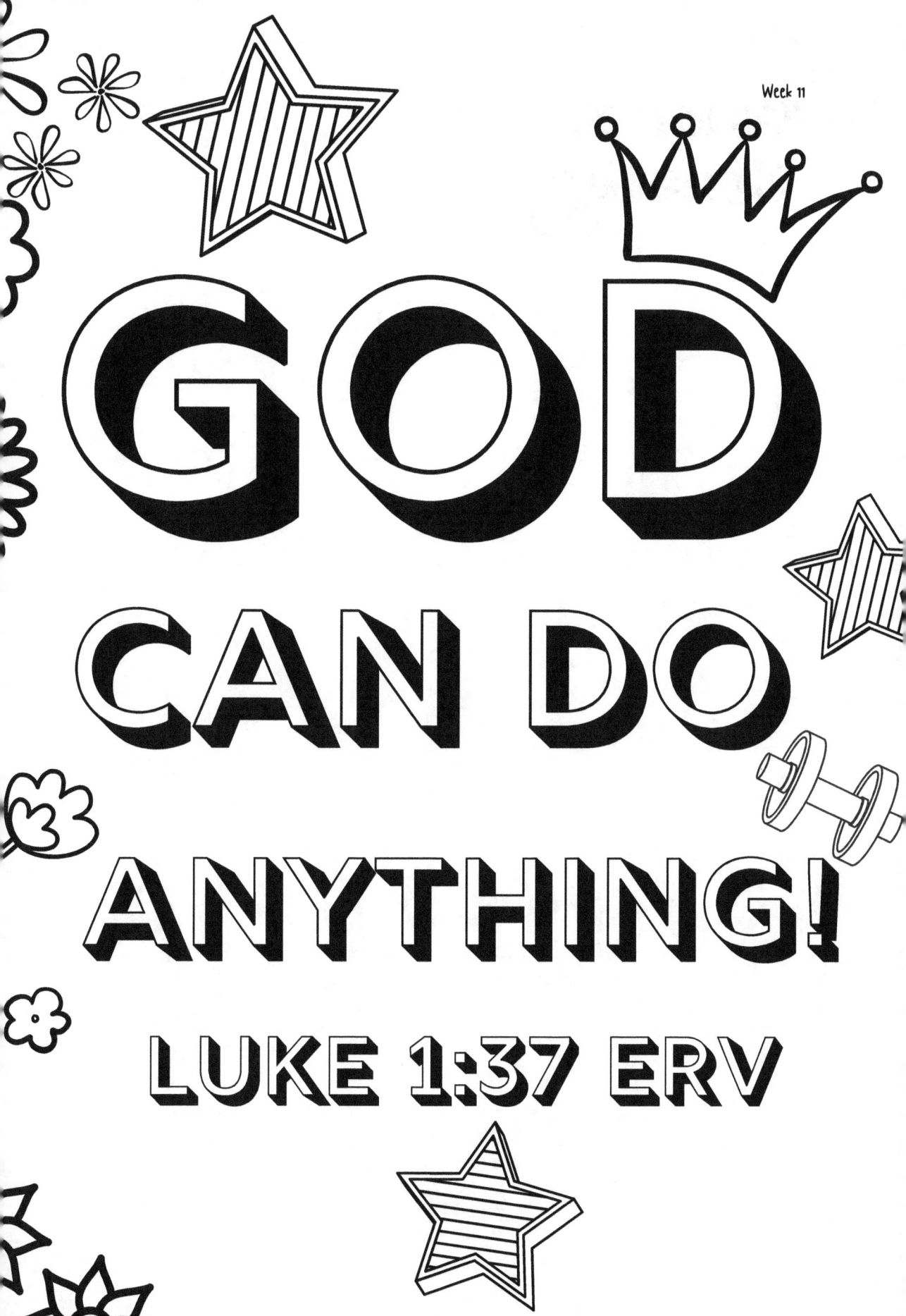

Week 12

I want my life and my words to spread the good news about Jesus

Week 12

SHARING THE GOOD NEWS

One of the last things Jesus said to his followers before He left the earth was to go and make more followers out of all the nations on earth. Knowing Jesus is good news and He wants us to share that news with everyone around us. We don't just do this with the words we say. We also tell the good news with the way we act, the way we love and the we care for others. We share the good news when we help people and show kindness. Even when we don't know what to do, the Holy Spirit in us helps us reflect the light of Jesus to the world around us. When we follow Jesus, and obey Him through our words and our lives, we point the way for others to know Him too. Everyone around us is invited to go to Jesus, be forgiven of their sins and have new life in Him!

Who in your life needs good news today?

Write Your Thoughts

_____

_____

_____

_____

 MONDAY | My Week | TUESDAY

WEDNESDAY | THURSDAY

Bible Verse

So go and make followers of all people in the world. Baptize them in the name of the Father and the Son and the Holy Spirit.
Matthew 28:19 ERV

FRIDAY

SATURDAY

SUNDAY

SAMARITAN WOMAN
The one who shared good news
John 4:1-41

There was a woman from a place called Samaria that had made many mistakes in her life. Jesus went out of his way to meet her, sitting at the well she visited to draw water. After talking to her about her life and about what it meant to know God, she realized that Jesus was the Messiah. He was the one that she had been waiting for all her life.

She knew that even though she had made many wrong choices, Jesus was the choice that would never go away or run out. After meeting Jesus she ran all the way back to her town and told everyone about Him. Because she shared this good news, many people in her town became followers of Jesus. **What are ways that you can share what Jesus has done in your life?**

Write Your Thoughts

_____

_____

_____

_____

_____

THE SAMARITAN WOMAN SPREAD THE GOOD NEWS TO EVERYONE IN HER TOWN!

Week 12

Jesus is

Good News

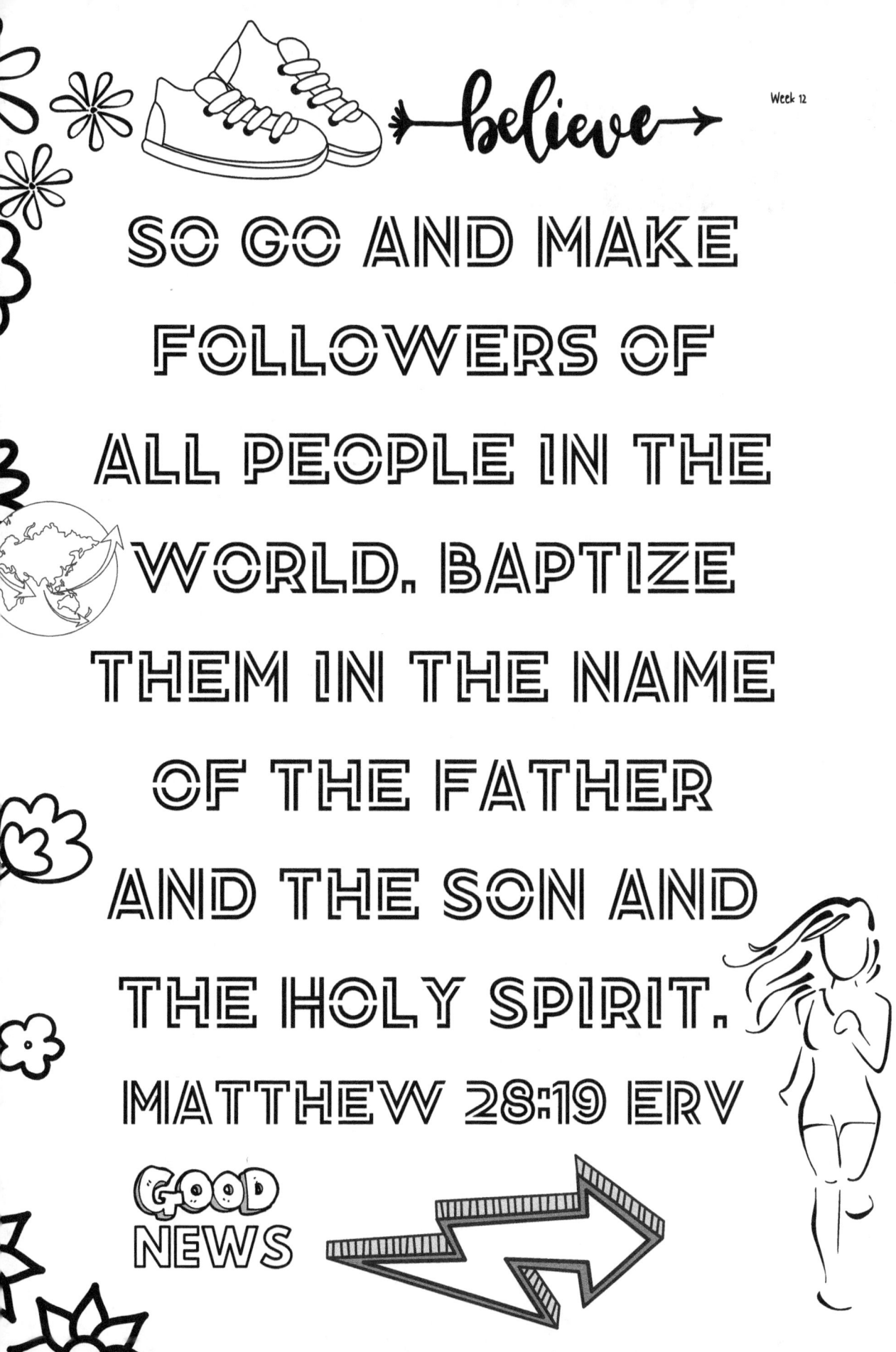

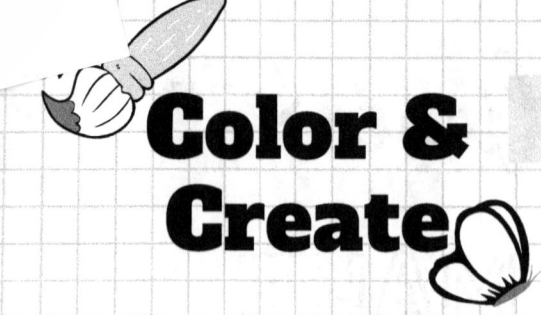

MORE RESOURCES!

BOOKS

- Milk & Honey in the Land of Fire & Ice
- Becoming His: Finding Your Place as a Daughter of God

JOURNALS & PLANNERS

- The Daddy's Boy Devotional
- Milk & Honey Women Study & Prayer Journal
- The Cultivational Planner: A Devotional Planner for Women
- Dwell: Bible Study & Prayer Journal
- Milk & Honey Women Devotional Journal

WE ARE ALWAYS COMING OUT WITH NEW RESOURCES, INCLUDING MORE FOR KIDS! SIGN UP AT WWW.MILKANDHONEYBOOKS.COM FOR INFO AND FREEBIES!

About the Author/Designer

Jenny Erlingsson is wife to her amazing viking husband and mother to four cute and fierce mocha drops. After over twelve years of serving in pastoral ministry in Alabama, she and her family currently live in Iceland working in various areas of ministry. Jenny is passionate about empowering others, especially women through her writing and speaking. She is also the author of **Milk & Honey in the Land of Fire & Ice** and **Becoming His: Finding Your Place as a Daughter of God**

More at WWW.MILKANDHONEYBOOKS.COM

www.ingramcontent.com/pod-product-compliance
Lightning Source LLC
Chambersburg PA
CBHW051805100526
44592CB00016B/2575